AF423171

Models in Mind
The Mind of Gorgias and Protagoras

Giacomo Piccinelli

FormAI
Publications

Models in Mind is a series of short publications focusing on the contributions
to the theory of mind and intelligence made by thinkers of all times.

The preliminary plan for the series includes:

The Mind of Pythagoras

The Mind of Parmenides

The Mind of Zeno

The Mind of Empedocles

The Mind of Gorgias and Protagoras

The Mind of Heraclitus

The Mind of Anaxagoras

The Mind of Democritus

The Mind of Plato

The Mind of Aristotle

The Mind of Plotinus

The Mind of Augustine

The Mind of Aquinas

The Mind of Leibnitz

The Mind of Kant

The Mind of Hegel

The Mind of Husserl

The Mind of Piaget

The Mind of Vygotsky

The Mind of Turing

The Mind of Minsky

Synthetic Thought

The latest information on the series can be found at:

https://www.FormAI.org

To Fausto

Not he who knows many things is wise,
but he who knows what is profitable.

(Aeschylus)

Preface

In the preliminary sections of Plato's Gorgias, Socrates encourages his interlocutors to be concise in the expression of their arguments. Gorgias not only agrees, within the limits of the possible, but also prides himself of being better than most at summarising complex arguments. Protagoras demonstrates an equal ability.

In addition to a spurious contrast between philosophy and sophistry, widespread theories position Gorgias and Protagoras in opposition to the Pythagoreans and, in particular, the Eleatics. We instead propose that in his dialogue "On What is Not" Gorgias schematically represents the doctrines of his predecessors, namely Xenophanes and Parmenides. Protagoras's dictum "Man is measure of all things" can be interpreted in a similar vein. In essence, however useful, knowledge and opinions are human constructs, bearing no necessary relation to reality.

Empedocles reminds us that by Water we understand water. Gorgias, with a more complete reference to Parmenides, also reminds us that by "water" we communicate Water, not water. Protagoras reminds us that Water is a human choice, not a necessity stemming from water.

G. P.

Acknowledgements

The book would not have been possible without the reference material and the inspiring work of many distinguished scholars, including but not limited to J. Barnes, R. Bett, F. M. Cornford, G. Clark, K. Craik, B. Croce, P. Duhem, P. Feyerabend, K. W. C. Guthrie, N. R. Hanson, G. E. R. Lloyd, K. Pearson, J. E. Raven, M. Schofield, and W. D. Woodhead.

Contents

The Mind of Gorgias and Protagoras

Introduction

Sophistry, like philosophy, has received different connotations over time. Originally, sophistry was intended as mastery of the wisdom of the human mind; with an emphasis on language as the mechanism to influence the mind. Associated arts, such as oratory and rhetoric, focused on the knowledge of the use language for expressing one's opinions and for changing the opinions held by others. Not surprisingly, such arts can be used for good as well as for evil purposes. Looking at examples in Plato's dialogue between Socrates and Gorgias, a physician can use language to persuade a reticent patient to undergo a life-saving procedure. Equally, unscrupulous individuals, with a better mastery of language, may persuade the administrators of a city to follow a course of action on public health different from the recommendations of an expert physician.

Some indications on the historical connection between sophistry and philosophy can be found in Plato's Protagoras, where Protagoras seems to refer to the Pythagoreans as the original sophists. According to Protagoras, the "old sophists" focused on arithmetic, geometry, music, and astronomy; the Pythagorean quadrivium. After a suitable induction, most Pythagoreans were known to take leadership positions in city governance. Hence, the possible emphasis on political influence attached to later notions of sophistry. The positive connotations of influencing by dialogue and argument rather than force are somehow underplayed, and sophistry seems to become predominantly linked to self-interested manipulation based on illusion and other kinds of linguistic trickery. Being at is may, the fundamentals of sophistry were and remain essential elements of architectural frameworks and meta-models for the mind.

The time (late 5th to early 4th century BCE) and location (Sicily) of Gorgias' formation are such that Pythagorean and, in particular, Eleatic influences appear inescapable. Especially accepting the hypothesis that Gorgias was a student of Empedocles, the connections with the doctrine of Parmenides and the methodology of Zeno can be easily traced. The connections with Pythagoras and Xenophanes are also apparent. The initial sections of this book outline the philosophical thought of these giants, with the intent of recreating a perspective as close as possible to the view afforded to Gorgias by Empedocles. Given the interactions between Italians and Greeks, the cultural context also applies to Protagoras.

The interpretation of the three-step argument proposed by Gorgias in "On What Is Not" occupies the central part of the book. The argument is reconstructed from an interpolation of the two canonical sources: "Against the Logicians" by Sextus Empiricus (ref. Empiricus S. and Bett R., 2005) and "On Melissus, Xenophanes, and Gorgias" by Pseudo-Aristotle (ref. Barnes J., 1984). The reference material for Protagoras is from the same book of Sextus Empiricus. The material on Protagoras is more limited in quantity than the material on Gorgias, but the limitation is more than compensated by the clarity of expression. Plato's three dialogues on Gorgias, Protagoras, and the Sophist (ref. Hamilton E. and Huntington C., 1982) provide useful context for both Gorgias and Protagoras.

In essence, we propose that the arguments of both Gorgias and Protagoras are representations and reflections on the triangle Nature–Mind–Language formalised by Parmenides (ref. Piccinelli, 2022).

Pythagoras

Folk lore depicts Pythagoras as the charismatic founder of a mystical religious cult, practicing selective vegetarianism and worshiping numbers, geometric figures, music, and stars. Admission to the cult was apparently based on a very selective process, which included a probationary period of induction lasting up to five years, with no guarantee of admission at the end. The doctrines of the cult were not put in writing. They were transmitted only orally, using an esoteric and highly metaphoric language. The sharing of the doctrines outside the cult was strictly forbidden. However, over time some of the content was exposed. The doctrine of immortality and transmigration of the soul was among those that most stimulated the general imagination. Pythagoras' interest in philosophy and cosmology also stimulated the imagination of the most learned among his contemporaries and their successors.

We propose that one of the best tools to reconcile fiction with facts is the biography of Pythagoras produced by Iamblichus (ref. Clark, 1989). When Pythagoras arrives in Italy, he carries extensive experience of Greek culture and, most importantly, of the cultures of Egypt and the Middle East. The experience is not limited to specific scientific notions. Notably, Pythagoras had been exposed to the lengthy processes of induction of the Egyptian religious orders. He has a deep understanding of the necessity of an education process that develops the individual gradually and as a whole. New notions can be absorbed only if (1) the mind has acquired the processes to manage an overall system of knowledge, (2) the principles on which the new notions are based have been established, and (3) other notions on which the new notions depend have also been established. The sequencing is essential. If general mental processes are not established, knowledge principles don't have an operating platform. If dependent notions are not properly interconnected, knowledge becomes fragmented. Either way, the mind will not be able to extract effective models of the world from the influx of sensory experience.

The emphasis on oral tradition is driven by the need to ensure that the learner is suitably guided by the teacher through the learning process, rather than being left to make assumptions on the interpretation of a book. Mistakes at one level weaken the foundations for subsequent levels. The seemingly jealous guarding of the doctrines is mainly driven by concerns for their comprehension. The risk is that, without the required foundations, the description of a doctrine may be misinterpreted. There is no evidence of elitism in the admission to the induction program. However, individuals that have not received the required training are not in a position to comprehend systematic principles and related notions. Language is instrumental to the development of knowledge, but words can be associated to different meanings, with profound consequences.

The doctrine of immortality and transmigration of the soul is a good example of the misunderstanding that can emerged from sharing the words but not the meanings underpinning a language. Indicatively, for Pythagoras the notion of a soul can be equated to the notion of the mental essence of an individual. The mind encompasses knowledge and opinion. Knowledge is a relatively static metamodel that can be applied to the world. Opinion captures a dynamic model of the world that an individual mind develops and maintains, based on knowledge and the ongoing influx of sensory experience. The essence of an individual is equated to the knowledge of the individual. As such, it is possible for the soul to move from one individual to another, as well as to survive the physical demise of the individual. One may or may not accept these notions, or the broader system of notions on which they depend. However, there is no religious mysticism involved. Drawing a parallel with Thales, Anaximander, or Anaximenes, there is a defined system of notions that, as such, can and should be judged based on the outcomes for the society of individuals that adopt the system.

An even more emblematic example of misunderstanding concerns the doctrine that "the world is made of numbers". Illustrious contemporaries such as Aristotle and, to a degree, Plato took Pythagorean references to numbers as to the common system of signs used for quantification and related computations. Such interpretation led to incomprehension and paradoxes that have persisted to modern times. Indicatively, Pythagorean numbers should be interpreted first and foremost as the principles underpinning the universe and, therefore, underpinning the mental models of the universe. Particular importance is attributed to four principles: (1) unity, (2) opposition, (3) the three-phased process of birth, life, and death, and (4) symmetry. For Pythagoras, what is normally referred to as mathematics or number theory is the theory of the unit(s). Geometry is the theory of the possible relations between units. Music, or harmony, is the theory of the desirable relations between units. Astronomy, or cosmology, is the theory of the actual relations between units. Traditional numbers can be derived from higher level principles and related metamodels. Traditional numbers, with their power of abstraction, are also likely to have provided inspiration for the higher-level principles. However, when Pythagoras maintains that the world is made of numbers, the reference is to the principles of the order (cosmos) for the universe (cosmos).

As final aspect in this cursory overview of Pythagoras, we must consider the notion of divinity. Especially if coming from monotheistic cultures, the notion of divinity may take connotations of absolute and universal power. Apart from initial calls from individuals such as Xenophanes, practically all religions at the time of Pythagoras were polytheistic. Hierarchies were in place, and gods at different levels had different powers and accountabilities. For Pythagoras, the notion of divinity is mainly associated to creative power. The hierarchy of divinity is the hierarchy of the cosmic principles, as they hold the creative power in the universe and in the mind. On a line of thought similar to the Ionian physicists, traditional religious and mythological systems are replaced with a non-anthropomorphic explanatory system for the universe. Combining the doctrine of divinity with the doctrine of the soul, we see how individuals, as systems of knowledge principles, can attract attributes of divinity.

In summary, the picture of Pythagoras painted by folklore may be seen as correct. However, the words must be attached to a very different semantics to obtain a meaningful interpretation.

Xenophanes

Despite the limited and fragmentary sources, Xenophanes emerges as an insightful thinker, well aligned with both the Ionian and Pythagorean philosophical traditions. For Xenophanes, the natural world has been created by divinity based on a logic that is neither accessible nor usable by humans (ref. Guthrie, 1962). Divinity is incommensurable with humanity in terms of resources, power, and knowledge. Humans must focus on developing knowledge and opinions that are more suitable to their abilities and circumstances. Even when divine logic and human logic are somehow aligned, they remain incommensurable.

Xenophanes maintained that humans' attribution of anthropomorphic characteristics to divinity is misguided, if intended as an attempt to establish a common ground with divinity. Humans may find it natural to attribute human characteristics to divinity. Horses would find it natural to attribute equine characteristics to divinity. While both humans and horses would be misguided in assuming that such characteristics are actual characteristics of divinity, both humans and horses can be justified in adopting models of divinity to which they can directly relate. The articulation of the doctrine is simple, but the philosophical implications concerning both the scope and the relativity of epistemology are powerful.

It is unclear whether the notion of the "one God" attributed to Xenophanes is a metaphor for the Pythagorean principle referred to as "oneness", "unity", or "the one and the many". However, the notional alignment seems highly likely. Equally likely is the convergence of thought in Xenophanes' epistemic notions linked to the indefinite dyad. Indicatively, it is useful for humans to have in their knowledge the concept of Sweetness defined as a range between two extremes. It is also useful for humans, to build opinions of Sweetness by pegging the extremes to clear reference points. For example, the flavour of ripe figs can be used as the upper limit. However, while knowledge should remain stable, opinions should be adjusted when appropriate. In the example, after the discovery of yellow honey the upper limit for the opinion of Sweetness should be changed from ripe figs to yellow honey. Knowledge is absolute, options relative to experience.

Xenophanes' apparent attribution of knowledge to divinity and of opinion to humanity can interpreted in two ways. Within a religious framework, the distinction reiterates the incommensurability of divinity and humanity, as well as the superiority of divinity to humanity. Stability is positioned as a divine prerogative, in contrast to constant change for the material world and humanity. Whitin a philosophical framework, the distinction highlights the difference between principles (e.g.: the definition of meta-models) and the application of principles (e.g.: the definition of models based on meta-models). The distinction bears strong resemblance with the Pythagorean doctrine and more esoteric practices, whereby, given their creative power, principles are attributed with divine status.

The connection between religious and philosophical frameworks is a double-edged sword. On the positive side, religious concepts can provide "intuition pumps" (ref. Dennett, 2013) as sources of conceptual patterns and structures. Religious metaphors and language can also be used for explanatory purposes. On a more dubious side, especially in the culture of Xenophanes' time, religious language could be used as a mechanism for persuasion, to give spurious authority to arguments. On the negative side, especially in the absence of a philosophical perspective on religion, the connection may become a source of confusion and friction. The resulting issues are exemplified by the misrepresentation of the Pythagoreans as a religious sect and related consequences. On balance, Xenophanes appears to benefit from the interplay of religion and philosophy.

Parmenides

As discussed in more detail in *The Mind of Parmenides* (ref. Piccinelli, 2022), Parmenides' focus is on the architecture of the mind. In particular, the problems addressed by Parmenides concern the best way for the human mind to think and build opinions as models of the real world. The world is structurally complex and in constant change. The mind is limited in its capacity to store information and its ability to process change. Models provide a pragmatic compromise between effectiveness and efficiency.

Parmenides proposes a mental architecture based on four main components: (P) Perception, (K) Knowledge, (T) Thought, and (O) Opinion (ref. Appendix A).

Perceptions represent, for the mind, the dynamics of the real world. They support rational thought and opinion as well as instincts. Instinctive processes focus on rapid response to the details of the here and now. Experience may result in adjustments to the processes, but no other memory is kept of the past. Rational thought and opinion take a broader perspective of the world, both spatially and temporally. The response is less rapid and precise, but it is more contextual. Both the processes and the context develop with experience. The models of the world useful for instincts are different from the models useful for opinions. However, both kinds of models derive, directly or indirectly, from perceptions and model the real world.

Parmenides proposes knowledge as a socially defined metamodel that thoughts must use for creating opinions, as models of the world. The metamodel must be assumed immutable and complete. If K changed, the system of opinions developed by an individual through experience would need to be adjusted. Moreover, the adjustment would need to be made by all the individuals in society. The assumption of completeness gives confidence to the individuals that they can understand the world without having to invent new concepts.

Knowledge is a systematic whole. Careless change can compromise its structural integrity. Most important, uncoordinated changes by individuals compromise social cohesion. The meaning of language is anchored to knowledge. Hence, one-sided changes to knowledge also erode the ability of individuals to communicate meaningfully.

Far from contemplating a material world in which change does not occur, Parmenides outlines a pragmatic solution for the mind to handle change in the world. The mind itself is supposed to change. However, a stable reference point enables consistency in the model of the world that the individual dynamically maintains. Having a common reference point, also enables individuals to operate as a society, which ultimately benefits the individuals.

The outline painted by Parmenides is drawn with bold lines for general consumption. As a constitutional lawyer, Parmenides has first-hand experience of the value of common principles and the benefits of stability. Equally, he has first-hand experience of the processes for the creation and maintenance of common principles. Parmenides also has first-hand experience of the power of religion. Hence, the religious metaphors deployed as a device for persuasion.

Zeno

The philosophy of Zeno of Elea is substantially that of Parmenides. As discussed in more detail in *The Mind of Zeno* (ref. Piccinelli, 2022), the famous paradoxes devised by Zeno were mainly intended to drive reflections on Parmenides's mental architecture. For reasons probably similar to those that led to the misinterpretation of Pythagoras, distorting representations of Parmenides' work were being circulated. In essence, the epistemological proposals of Parmenides were interpreted as physical proposals, which led to paradoxical conclusions. For example, the metaphor of the sphere intended to indicate the systematic character of knowledge was represented as a geometrical position on the physical world. Similarly, the notion that knowledge should be stable was represented as denial of change in the physical world.

Partially as a reaction to malicious attacks and partly in the hope to encourage reflection on genuine misunderstandings, Zeno constructed a number of arguments aimed at artificially driving paradoxical conclusions from the application of physical notions to the mental domain. For example, some concepts were made to exhibit a requirement of being infinitely large in size, which would apparently make it impossible for the concepts to fit in a mind of limited size, such as the mind of humans. Similar techniques were used to drive paradox in the case of the infinitely small. For example, in the famous case of Achilles and the tortoise.

Anticipating, among others, the pragmatists; Zeno drives reflection on the need for knowledge to be defined taking into consideration the domain of application, the characteristics of the user, and the value to the user.

Empedocles

Based on the available evidence, Empedocles was steeped in the Pythagorean and Eleatic philosophy (ref. Piccinelli, 2022). The structure of Empedocles' production can be divided in three parts: (1) general preparations for the mind to be able to receive knowledge and related opinions, (2) an introduction to the principles of knowledge and nature, and (3) specific scientific knowledge and opinions aligned with observation and the principles of knowledge and nature. In one of the fragments of his writings, he appears to confess to a major offence against the gods, for which the punishment is to be banished from their presence for a very long time. It is quite possible that the offence was precisely to have put in writing and to be spreading to uninitiated the Pythagorean doctrine.

Concerning nature, Empedocles proposes four physical principles: water, earth, air, and fire. In addition, Empedocles proposes the principles of composition and decomposition, poetically referred to as love and hate. New entities are created by composing pre-existing entities. The new entities exist for various amounts of time, depending on some logic of evolutionary fitness. Eventually entities are decomposed, to various degrees. Composition and decomposition are balanced and alternate in eternal cycles. The corresponding four principles of knowledge are the Pythagorean principles of unity, opposition, generation-existence-degeneration, and symmetry. The degree to which composition and decomposition were, at least implicitly, Pythagorean principles or a novel addition by Empedocles is difficult to assess and substantiate.

In terms of mental architecture, Empedocles is aligned with Parmenides (ref. Appendix B). Expressions along the lines of "by water we understand water" confirm the duality of nature and mind. The first instance of "water" is intended as the mental concept of Water, the second instance is intended as the material entity of water. The alignment between Empedocles and Parmenides is also apparent concerning perceptions. Material entities are modelled as producing "effluences" that interact with the sense organs of the body, which produces perceptions in the mind. However, "the [perception of] blackness from the bottom of a deep river is the same as the [perception of] blackness from a deep cavern". Perceptions must be judged based on knowledge to generate suitable opinions. Prior experience, captured by a system of opinions, also informs judgement. However, perceptions do not directly enter the system of opinions, let alone the system of knowledge.

As Empedocles had direct contact with Parmenides, and quite possibly with other Pythagoreans, the content of his writings provides a significant reference for the cultural background of Gorgias.

On What Is Not

The epistemology and broader metaphysics of Gorgias can be inferred from the testimonies on his work "On Nature" or, symmetrically, "On What Is Not" captured in Sextus Empiricus' "Against the Logicians" (ref. Empiricus and Bett, 2005) and in Pseudo-Aristotle's "On Melissus, Xenophanes, and Gorgias" (ref. Barnes, 1984). The two sources appear broadly aligned on the outline of the argument. However, both works show a substantial amount of interpretation and can only be treated as indicative. Most important, both works lack in the interpretative context, that we believe is essential to appreciate Gorgias' intent and message.

Based on the cultural background that Gorgias inherits from the Pythagoreans and, in particular, the Eleatics, we propose that his work should be interpreted mostly as an outline of the separation between the mental world and the physical world (see also Appendix C). In particular, Gorgias can be seen as building on the epistemological doctrines of Xenophanes and Parmenides (ref. Piccinelli, 2022). The choice of Melissus and, most importantly, Xenophanes as joint subjects with Gorgias by Pseudo-Aristotle is not without significance.

According to the two sources, Gorgias' argument unfolds in three main steps:

1. Nothing is.
2. If anything is, it cannot be grasped.
3. If anything is and can be grasped, it cannot be communicated.

Indicatively, we propose that the wording can expanded as:

1. Nothing is [known about reality].
2. [Even] if anything is [known about reality], it [reality] cannot be grasped [by the mind].
3. [Even] if anything is [known about reality] and [reality] can be grasped, it [the grasp on reality] cannot be communicated.

Again indicatively, we propose that the steps should be interpreted as follows:

1. However useful, the human mental logos (knowledge) is different from the physical logos. Hence, none of the "things" that exist in the mental world (opinions) has an exact counterpart in the physical world. For illustration: the human mind may find it useful to have a concept of Apple, and related opinions about apples in the world. However, purely to convey the sense of the argument, nature may simply see the apple of the mind as an aggregate of atoms. There are no apples for nature. With Parmenides, knowledge is a human construct.

2. Allowing for things of the mind (knowledge-based opinions) to match the things (objects) of the physical world, there is no "tangible" connection between opinions and objects. The mind may have opinions about there being apples on a tree and, in reality, apples may be on a tree. However, there is no tangible connection between the opinions of apples and the physical apples. A reason why, with Xenophanes, even when our opinions are true (as in "matching reality"), we cannot be certain that they are true.

3. Allowing for the connection between opinions and objects to have some kind of existence, one mind cannot communicate the connection to another mind, at least using language. Assuming, with Empedocles, the chain Object → Effluence → Influence (Perception) → Opinion, language can, at best, encode opinions. Language cannot encode perceptions. Hence, in speech-based communication, the connection between opinion of the mind and object of reality is lost.

In summary, the outline of the argument could be rephrased as:

1. Our opinions of reality do not match reality.
2. Even if our opinions matched reality, opinions cannot be linked to reality.
3. Even if we could link opinions to reality, we cannot communicate the link; at least using language.

Step 1

The first step is supported by a number of proofs that highlight the limitations of human knowledge. The inference that can be drawn is that such a weak logos cannot begin to match the logos underpinning the cosmos.

The first proof is an example of the structural inconsistency that human knowledge can exhibit. Based on the common notion of being as possession of characteristics, not being, as opposite of being, is taken as not having any characteristic. However, not having any characteristic can be taken as a characteristic, which triggers an apparent paradox (similar to "this is a lie" or the "barber" paradoxes addressed by Bertrand Russell). At the time of Gorgias, this "I am not" kind of paradoxes may be compared in effect to the discovery of irrational numbers (e.g. the square root of two). A reminder of the limits of human knowledge. Limits unlikely to apply to the natural logos.

The remaining proofs draw on the discordance between the main physical meta-models proposed at the time. Granting the possible consistency and validity of the individual doctrines, one is left with the need to reconcile the contradictions in their respective positions. In the examples provided by Gorgias, one needs to reconcile the doctrine that every thing is one with the doctrine that every thing is many, the doctrine that reality is generated with the doctrine that reality is un-generated, and the doctrine that change (including motion as change of position in space) is possible with the opposite position. As reconciliation appears impossible, one may be led to the inference that the domain to which the conflicting propositions apply must be empty; so that the tenets of classic logic are somehow preserved. However, a simpler explanation is that the conceptual principles and doctrines considered are not adequate to model reality.

Given the inadequacy of human knowledge, one would therefore be well advised not to expect the opinions on things held by the mind to actually match reality.

Step 2

Assuming that the mind has a valid system of knowledge for reality; the second step focuses on the link between opinions and reality. The surviving portion of the argument proceeds in two directions: (i) there are things in reality that do not exist in the mind, and (ii) there are things in the mind that do not exist in reality. Hence, there does not appear to be a necessary link between opinions and reality.

If there were a link between objects of reality and opinions, there would be no false opinions, which, experience suggests, is not the case. If objects of the mind were linked to objects on the world, somebody thinking about a chariot speeding away on the surface of the sea would imply the reality of the situation envisioned, which, experience suggests, is also not the case.

Gorgias draws an illustrative parallel with perceptions. Things are not more or less real because they are or are not seen. Equally, things are not more or less real because they or are not thought.

Step 3

The third and final step concerns linguistic communication. The implicit assumptions are: (i) with Empedocles, a chain Object $\rightarrow$ Effluence $\rightarrow$ Influence (Perception) $\rightarrow$ Opinion, and (ii) with Parmenides, that Knowledge provides the building blocks for Opinion, and Language is linked to Knowledge.

The argument is subdivided in two parts:

a) The sender of a message would not be able, using language, to encode the perceptual information T_{PS} on a thing T that the sender derived from the effluences of T. The sender could only encode the opinions associated to T_{PS}.

b) Even if the sender could pass T_{PS} on to the receiver, any receiver different from the sender would not be able to connect the information with T, because the mind of the received would have a different experience T_{RS} of T.

On the first point. The mind of the sender would have experienced a physical object T in terms of perceptions of, for example, colour and sound. Given that speech from the sender cannot recreate the same perceptions in the receiver, the mind of the receiver would not be able to recreate the understanding of T that the sender holds.

On the second point. For the mind of the receiver to understand that with T_P the sender is referring to T, the mind of the receiver should already have encountered T and formed an experience T_P of T. However, different individuals have different experiences of the same object. Hence, the mind of the receiver is likely to have an experience

T_{PR} associated with T. Unless T_{PR} is equal to T_{PS} the receiver will not understand, or be certain, that the sender is referring to T.

The receiver can understand the opinions of the sender. However, the receiver will not be able to connect with certainty the opinions of the sender with the reality from which the opinions were derived.

Considerations

In line with Parmenides, Gorgias presents human knowledge and opinion as, respectively, meta-model and model for a real world at which the mind can at best glimpse by perception. The mind can think and build opinions with what it knows (Parmenides' "what is and cannot not be"). Anything for which the mind does not have knowledge (Parmenides' "what is not and must not be") for the mind does not exist. However, mental existence does not imply or depend upon physical existence.

In line with Xenophanes, the principles of knowledge on which opinions are built may coincide with the principles on which physical objects are built, but the coincidence is neither a necessity nor a certainty. Two systems can only be related in a super-system. Truth, as relation between the mind and the world, is not accessible to the mind. The mind can at most draw relations between different conceptual representations of the world. Hence, the truthfulness of any mental proof of existence is illusory.

We may understand water (a physical object) by Water (a mental object), and by "water" (item of language) we may communicate Water (a mental object). However, we could equally well understand water (a physical object) by Transparent+Liquid (a combination of mental objects) and communicate the concept Transparent+Liquid by the word "eau" (item of language). Physical objects and perceptions are independent from knowledge, opinions, and language.

On Measure

The epistemological position of Protagoras is often summarised as "Man is the measure of all things". However, the extended version of the position reported, among others, by Sextus Empiricus in "Against the Logicians" (ref. Empiricus and Bett, 2005) brings additional clarity and ease of traceability:

"Man is the measure of all things. Of things that are, that they are. Of things that are not, that they are not."

Taking "measure" in the sense of device for rationalisation or mental meta-model, the alignment with Parmenides' doctrine appears fairly clear. Indicatively, Parmenides maintained that "what is" (i) is, (ii) is the object of thought, and (iii) gives meaning to what we talk about. In essence, (i) the capability of the mind to build models of the world is determined by the system of knowledge, (ii) we can build opinions only based on knowledge, and (iii) the meaning of language is anchored to knowledge. Conversely, "what is not" (i) is not, (ii) cannot be thought, and (iii) cannot be communicated. In essence, (i) what we don't have knowledge of, for the mind cannot exist, (ii) we cannot maintain opinions about it, and (iii) we cannot talk about it. Moreover, Parmenides firmly positioned knowledge as a social standard. For a society, "what is" is what the society choses it to be. For example, a society may choose to have horses and zebras, or to just have horses with different patterns of colour. In the second case, for the mind, zebras simply do not exist.

Protagoras' dictum provides a very effective summary of Parmenides' doctrine. Society chooses the mental structures with which its members model the world. Structures may be more or less useful or easy to use. However, the mental logos remains a social choice, both in terms of elements and relations. Different individuals may have different opinions; for example, based on different experiences. However, all opinions should be built on the same knowledge; so that they can be effectively communicated and compared. Discussing measurements based on incommensurable measures may not be particularly productive.

The position that Protagoras takes on gods (ref. Diogenes Laertius as reported in Hicks, 2015) provides an illuminating example of the relation between knowledge and existence:

"... concerning gods, I do not know whether they do or do not exist, and, if they do exist, which are their shapes. Countless impediments lay on the way to their knowledge: in particular, the poor illumination and the short extent of man's life"

In alignment with Gorgias, knowledge drives mental existence. However, mental existence and existence in the physical, divine, and possibly other realms cannot be determined by the mind or, at least, not by the human mind.

On Truth and What May Be

Both Gorgias and Protagoras build on the Milesian and Pythagorean insights into the distinction between mental and other realms. The important reminder that they provide is that the models of the world on which the traditional notion of truth is based are also mental models, derived from applying the specific meta-models to experience; directly or indirectly. For example, atomic physics may offer a specific view of the world, but it remains a conceptual view.

Access to truth as correspondence between a mental system of opinions and the system of nature is not possible for the mind. What may be possible is to establish a correspondence between different system of opinions; for example, tracing the opinions of an individual and the opinions of particular individuals (e.g. "experts"). There is no denial of the possibility or value of social standards. However, at least people that hold governance roles in society, should not forget (i) how given standards came to be and (ii) that it may sometime be useful for standards to change.

In Plato's Phaedrus, Socrates appears to disparage Gorgias for favouring a notion of truth based on logic consistency over a notion of truth based on correspondence to reality. The criticism seems to be based on a misunderstanding of feasibility for desirability. Gorgias is not denying the value in the knowledge of the logos of nature; he is simply sceptical that such knowledge is possible, at least for the human mind. Plato proposes a cosmology whereby gods create and operate the world based on a divine logos; a logos to which the human mind is exposed before being implanted, with the rest of the soul, into the human body. Under such assumptions, Gorgias would have probably agreed that the mind should strive to recover the divine logos and use it as the standard on which to build and judge opinions about the world. However, for all its elegance, Plato's cosmology is a mental construct for which the mind has no way to validate correspondence with a physical or divine reality.

Conclusions

Taking wisdom as the system of principles underpinning the architecture of the mind, the distinction between philosophy and sophistry becomes one of emphasis more than substance. Pythagoras referred to himself as a philosopher ("lover" of wisdom) as a reminder that sophistry (the "mastery" of wisdom) is an aspirational target to work towards with commitment and dedication, rather than a well-defined result of a well-defined process. The struggle in Plato's Sophist to draw a distinction between a sophist and a philosopher bears witness to the artificial nature of the distinction, and to the confusion of practice with practitioner. There may well be issues with specific rhetoricians or rhetoric arguments, but they should not be confused with issues of rhetoric as science, art, or even craft. Even accepting a Platonic re-connotation of sophistry and philosophy, the relevance of both Gorgias and Protagoras to philosophy is much greater than that of quite a number of the philosophers that disparaged them.

Gorgias and Protagoras promote the main tenets of Parmenides and the wider Pythagorean doctrine of the mind. Gorgias may be seen as focusing on the negative implications of the doctrine. Nature is inaccessible to the mind. We can build conceptual systems that help rationalise and communicate possible models of the world. However, the human mind has no way of tracing the correspondence between mental objects and physical objects. Protagoras may be seen as focussing on the positive implications of the doctrine. Humans are in control of the mental world. The mind can decide the structure to impose on the world, including what can and cannot be deemed to exist.

Gorgia and Protagoras remind us that the reality against which truth assessments can be made by the mind is a defined system of opinions based on a defined system of knowledge. Both systems are defined by social processes for, as Plato would say, the good of society. Both systems can evolve.

Appendix A: Parmenides' AoM

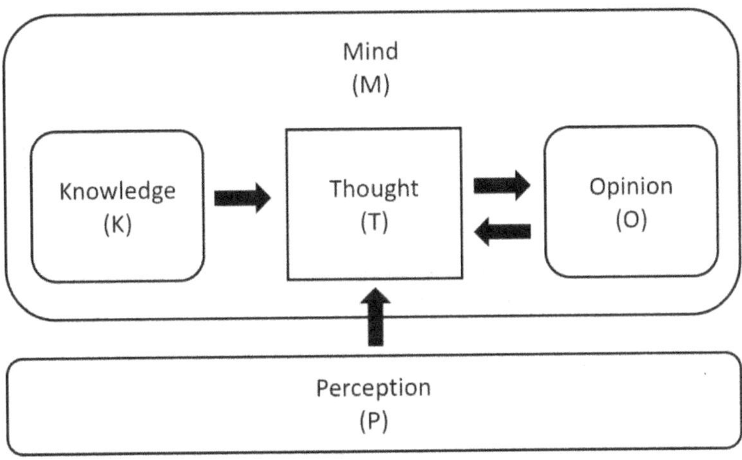

Schematic architecture of the Mind for Parmenides and Zeno:

- Knowledge primes Thought.
- Perceptions enter the Mind via Thought.
- Thoughts leverage Knowledge and extant Opinions for processing the flow of Perceptions and evolve Opinions.
- Thoughts can also evolve Opinions independently from Perception.
- Language is connected to Knowledge, hence to Opinions.

Appendix B: Empedocles' AoM

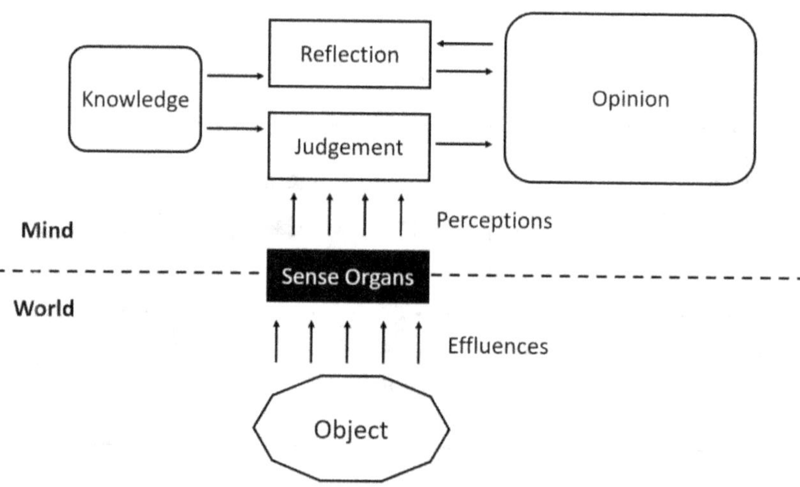

Schematic architecture of the Mind for Empedocles:

- Objects of the World produce various kinds of effluences. For example: light, vibrations, and heat.
- The sense organs react to the effluences from the objects and produce various kinds of perceptions. For example: perceptions of colours, perceptions of sounds, and perceptions of temperature.
- Judgement, based on Knowledge, detects patterns of perceptions, and produces corresponding opinions. For example: the opinions of Yellow and Bright, the opinion of Silent, the opinion of Hot, and the opinion of Sun.
- Reflection, based on Knowledge and Opinion, produces new opinions or modifies existing opinions. For example, given a pre-existing opinion of Cellar, it may change the opinion of Sun into the opinions of Light Bulb.

Note: The objects of the mind do not share the nature of the objects of the world. For example, the opinion of Sun qua opinion bears no resemblance with the Sun qua material object.

Appendix C: Gorgias' Synthesis

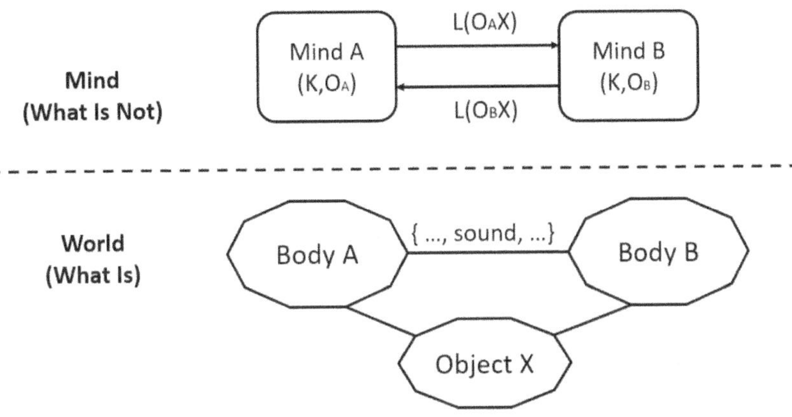

Gorgias' synthesis:

- The meta-model (knowledge) that the human mind uses to model (opinion) the world is not necessarily aligned to the natural logos; human knowledge is a (social) construct of the human mind.
- Assuming alignment between mental and natural logos, there is no necessary link between mental opinions and world objects. Opinions and objects can exist independently from each other.
- Assuming that a link exists between an opinion and an object (e.g. based on Empedocles' chain Object → Effluence → Influence (Perception) → Opinion), language can encode and speech can convey the opinion, but not the link.

When considering notions such as Reality and Truth, humans should be mindful of the limitations of tools at their disposal (knowledge, opinions, and language).

Bibliography

Anderson J. R. (1983) *The Architecture of Cognition.* Lawrence Erlbaum Associates, Inc.

Ambrose V. (2021) *The Fragments of Parmenides and Heraclitus.* Bishop & Hudson.

Austin S. (2007) *Parmenides and the History of Dialectic: Three Essays.* Parmenides Publishing.

Barnes J. (Ed.) (1984) *The Complete Works of Aristotle.* Princeton University Press.

Barnes J. (2001) *Early Greek Philosophy.* Penguin Group.

Barnet J. (1920) *Early Greek Philosophy.* Adam & Charles Black.

Bruner J. S., Goodnow J. J. and Austin G. A. (1986) *A Study of Thinking.* Routledge.

Brunshwig J. and Lloyd G. E. R. (2000) *Greek Thought.* Harvard University Press.

Clark G. (1989) *Iamblichus: On the Pythagorean Life.* University of Liverpool Press.

Cordero N. L. (2004) *By Being, It Is.* Parmenides Publishing.

Cornford F. M. (1912) *From Religion to Philosophy.* Longmans, Green and Co.

Cornford F. M. (1939) *Plato and Parmenides.* Kegan Paul, Trench, Trubner & Co.

Craik K. (1967) *The Nature of Explanation.* Cambridge University Press.

Croce B. (1917) *Logic as the Science of Pure Concept.* MacMillan and Co.

Croce B. (1921) *The Essence of Aesthetics.* William Heinemann.

Curd P. (2004) *The Legacy of Parmenides*. Parmenides Publishing.

Dennett D. (2013) *Intuition Pumps and Other Tools for Thinking*. Penguin Publishing.

Empiricus S. (Auth.) and Bett R. (Ed./Tr.) (2005) *Against the Logicians*. Cambridge University Press.

Fine G. (Ed.) (1999) *Plato 1. Metaphysics and Epistemology*. Oxford University Press.

Fine G. (Ed.) (1999) *Plato 2. Ethics, Politics, Religion and the Soul*. Oxford University Press.

Feyerabend P. (1975) *Against Method*. New Left Books.

Gallop D. (1984) *Parmenides of Elea*. University of Toronto Press.

Geldard R. (2007) *Anaxagoras and Universal Mind*. Ralph Waldo Emerson Institute Books.

Graham D. W. (2010) *The Texts of Early Greek Philosophy*. Cambridge University Press.

Guthrie K. W. C. (1962) *A History of Greek Philosophy, Volume I: The Earlier Presocratics and the Pythagoreans*. Cambridge University Press.

Guthrie K. W. C. (1965) *A History of Greek Philosophy, Volume II: The Presocratic Tradition from Parmenides to Democritus*. Cambridge University Press.

Guthrie K. W. C. (1971) *A History of Greek Philosophy, Volume III: The Fifth-Century Enlightenment – Part 1: The Sophists; Part 2: Socrates*. Cambridge University Press.

Hanson N. R. (1958) *Patterns of Discovery*. Cambridge University Press.

Hamilton E. and Huntington C. (Ed.) (1982) *Plato: The Collected Dialogues*. Princeton University Press.

Hicks R. D. (2015) *Complete Works of Diogenes Laertius*. Delphi Publishing Ltd.

Hopper V. F. (1938) *Medieval Number Symbolism.* Columbia University Press.

Inwood B. (2001) *The Poem of Empedocles.* University of Toronto Press.

Jaynes J. (1976) *The Origin of Consciousness in the Breakdown of the Bicameral Mind.* Mariner Books.

Johnson-Laird P. N. (1983) *Mental Model.* Cambridge University Press.

Kahn C. H. (2001) *Pythagoras and the Pythagoreans.* Hackett Publishing Company, Inc.

Kahn C. H. (2009) *Essays on Being.* Oxford University Press.

Kingsley P. (1995) *Ancient Philosophy, Mystery and Magic. Empedocles and the Pythagorean Tradition.* Clarendon Press.

Kirk, G. S., Raven J. E. and Schofield M. (2013) *The Presocratic Philosophers.* Cambridge University Press.

Lesher J. H. (2008) 'The Humanizing of Knowledge in Presocratic Thought'. *The Oxford Handbook of Presocratic Philosophy.* Oxford University Press.

Lloyd G. E. R. (1966) *Polarity and Analogy.* Cambridge University Press.

Lloyd G. E. R. (1979) *Magic, Reason and Experience.* Cambridge University Press.

Lloyd G. E. R. (1990) *Demystifying Mentalities.* Cambridge University Press.

Macphail E. M. (1998) *The evolution of Consciousness.* Oxford University Press.

McKirahan R. (2008) 'Signs and Arguments in Parmenides B8'. *The Oxford Handbook of Presocratic Philosophy.* Oxford University Press.

Lee H. D. P. (1967) *Zeno of Elea.* Adolf M. Hakkert.

Long A. A. (1986) *Hellenistic Philosophy.* Gerald Duckworth and Co. Ltd.

O'Brien D. (1969) *Empedocles' Cosmic Cycle.* Cambridge University Press.

Palmer J. (2012) *Parmenides and Presocratic Philosophy.* Oxford University Press.

Piccinelli, G. (2022) *The Mind of Parmenides.* FormAI Publications.

Piccinelli, G. (2022) *The Mind of Zeno.* FormAI Publications.

Piccinelli, G. (2022) *The Mind of Empedocles.* FormAI Publications.

Prier R. A. (1976) *Archaic Logic: Symbol and Structure in Heraclitus, Parmenides and Empedocles.* Mouton & Co.

Popper K. (1988) *The World of Parmenides.* Routledge.

Ogden C. K. and Richards I. A. (1927) *The Meaning of Meaning.* Harcourt, Brace and Company, Inc.

Osborne, C. (2004) *Presocratic Philosophy.* Oxford University Press.

Owen G. E. L. (1960) 'Eleatic Questions.' *The Classical Quarterly*, 10-1: 84-102. Cambridge University Press.

Sassure, F. d. and Harris R. (Ed./Tr.) (2013) *Course in General Linguistics.* Bloomsbury Publishing Plc.

Simplicius (Auth.), Huby P. (Tr.) and Taylor C. C. W. (Tr.) (2011) *On Aristotle Physics 1.3-4.* Bloomsbury.

Snell B. (1953) *The Discovery of the Mind.* Harvard University Press.

Thanassas P. (1967) *Parmenides, cosmos, and being: a philosophical interpretation.* Marquette University Press.

Tomasello M. (1999) *The Cultural Origins of Human Cognition.* Harvard University Press.

Trepanier S. (2004) *Empedocles: An Interpretation.* Routledge.

Turing A. M. (1950) 'Computing Machinery and Intelligence.' *Mind*, 236: 433-460.

Vlastos G. (1995) *Studies in Greek Philosophy. Vol.1: The Presocratics*. Princeton University Press.

Vlastos G. (1995) *Studies in Greek Philosophy. Vol.2: Socrates, Plato and their Tradition*. Princeton University Press.

Waterfield R. (1988) *The Theology of Arithmetic*. Phanes Press.

Waterfield R. (2000) *The First Philosophers*. Oxford University Press.

Wright M. R. (1981) *Empedocles: The Extant Fragments*. Yale University Press.

Zeller E. (1889) *Outlines of the History of Greek Philosophy*. Henry Holt and Co.

FormAI
Publications

www.ingramcontent.com/pod-product-compliance
Lightning Source LLC
Chambersburg PA
CBHW072127150726
47999CB00005B/2176